Weird-Heavy

Jesus Solis-Leon

BookLeaf Publishing

India | USA | UK

Presentation by *BookLeaf Publishing*

Web: www.bookleafpub.com

E-mail: info@bookleafpub.com

ISBN: 9789395088541

First edition 2022

DEDICATION

To versions of us, wading through the
weird-heavy feelings, who never got to be.

...

I see you.

...

Remember, rains will dissipate
and kingdoms to reign will come.

...

But all in due time.

...

<u>*Overwhelming Circumstance*</u>

'You, the first of your lineage to walk this path.'
Cheshire smile above the horizon reminds,
and I am petrified.

such	an	overwhelming	circumstance
~~and~~	+	~~am~~	~~petrified~~
~~and~~	+	~~am~~	~~petrified~~
~~and~~	+	~~am~~	~~petrified~~

like Jack - - ... - - ... - - I have drowned - - ... - - ... - - frozen in time ...
rose embroidery on blankets of depressive anxious thoughts and inequalities
presented to me ... - - on a near daily basis - - ... such an overwhelming
circumstance - - ... - - Father, maybe one day the pleas will work and
I'll be heard - no matter the outcome I won't be hurt, by empty words

---

... - there 'll be empty tear-pockets, sure - when I get the urge to divulge -
...

'Make sense of it - -
    - - cuz *it's* all you have now - - - - - no kin to be found...
                        and
                        so very few
                        try to help
                        when
                        you
                        drown.'

.

.

.

<u>*Corrosive Silence*</u>

It's
crippling
the sound
of nothing –
corrosive
in its
silence.
removed of
breath, length, width, and
every possible dimension.
to mention anything
in her presence,
would be a sin.
a lonely snake
adorns her body,
making me quiver.
doe eyed,
she stares in my direction. immense,
the response of synapses
down my back as
achilles gets the memo.
snapping back,
her grace washes over
the moment –
my skin blistering
in condemnation.
I revel.
she is not
a friend,
nor is she a foe.
she is simply,
silence.
|
∧

...

<u>*Willow*</u>

                              willow
                          | weeping,|
                          | |
                          | why do you wallow
                          | in the breeze |like so?
                          | | anxious
                          | surrounded
                          by an overflow of s
              I | | a
            am | | d
             sorry | n
               your | e
               evolutionary | s
               | line | s
               | has done you in,
               | giving the burdens you uphold.
          paperweight, |
                 to state affairs |
          beyond your prowess. |
                 remember, |
          no matter where the breeze may blow,
                 | | your
                 | | leaves
                 | | and branches
          battle disallowance. |
          soon as you carry on, |
                 too, with the breeze
          they'll have to leave. |
                     | gone will be their judgment.
          gone will be control. |
               | gone will be the virtue that
               | they think they hold.
               | and you too will be free,
               | to sway | in the wind
               | as you please. |
               | |

<u>*Broken Boy*</u>

It felt wrong   on arrival. I see a
man whose method for survival, patching broken
bodies. We, secondary symptoms – to which existence
is primary. Not allowed to live in peace, but expected to
live in pieces. Boy weeping, a secondary symptom
to a fractured knee. How to explain pain only migrates,
like we do? From knee to belly, mind to heart, and spirit.
Over visas. On stolen land near givers of
disease. Where no given 's ever guaranteed.
Is brown skin, truly, the lack of us?
…enough… Keep sympathy you think you
give. It isn't I who need forgive,
sins carried out on the illegals.
Sympathy I give to you, for
praying to a god who
made and
perfected
my
people.

–
I've
grown –
tired of
hating
my
skin – –
Hating
my nose's
defining tip – –
The way   my
shoulders   chip –
Holding   every-
thing   within –
Expressing   as I
do
and   expecting
to only get,
whiteness
Preference
disguising self-hate

Oh, the sweet, sweet flavor of assimilation

…

I Stayed

Happy little accident
or an honest mistake?
Some days, I can't tell the two apart.
You tore me to pieces –
in silence
and I sit there,
watching.
Arms at my side,
hoping the next string pulled
would unravel your love for me.
I stayed   –   watching,
hoping you'd see
how much it hurt.
I stayed

...

quiet,
hoping my silence

I should feel it in my toes,
as the clothes roll off my body –
very few know surrender
like I'm willing to forego.
for you.

At a loss for words with you
I've noticed that divulging the truth
makes you timid too
so, if not for me or you,
then what exactly is *so* confusing?

I don't know what to do,
I know I can push through
I know that I can – should I choose to
should I choose me,
or can I march to my rhythm
and still choose you?

would be enough.
All you needed
to see the pain you caused.

I stayed,

then you left.

. . .

Was brown skin the lack of my enough?

Brag, about diamonds? When they're as
common as blood of the children who mine
them? Few seem   to mind - rather - comment,
on monopoly   design   for   disenfranchisement.
Instead, shine refractive   light on 'em. Lusting for
luster's man made disaster - chains of adamantine atop sterling
steeples. Bodies   stapled to the ground   beneath our
feet. Opened-pit,   stomachs feel   sickness rise and I
can't stomach   pacification.   One day we will
all return to dust and all   will once again
be equal. Remember, only gods can
sanctify.   So, please recognize
that.   One day we will all
return to dust and
all will once
again be
equal.

<u>*Expose*</u>

feel a
lump in my
throat. words pulling
the pulse. choking sounds,
like the deep   bellied
bellow   of a
frog –
breath
held high –
if it ever
were to stop,
a croak. there'd be a
scythe held high by a
cloak. part of my psyche
yearns   for the
hold   'cause
I'm   just as
sharp and
lanky as
the pole.
and I know
that it's dark,
wild, and loose
but daily, I
choose to
keep away
nooses and
booze.
the
control's
set on
cruise –
if I ever
were to
crash, I'd
bruise –
but I do refuse to lose. loss.
windows shattered. covered in glass, the soul is morose. many a
time I've been close to letting myself be engulfed, like oil spills in

my mother land's golf, I don't. all the life on my coast held in place by an anchor, like that of a boat. and I hope I don't bore, like holes I drill into trenches of myself – digging deeper – and yet again,   expose.

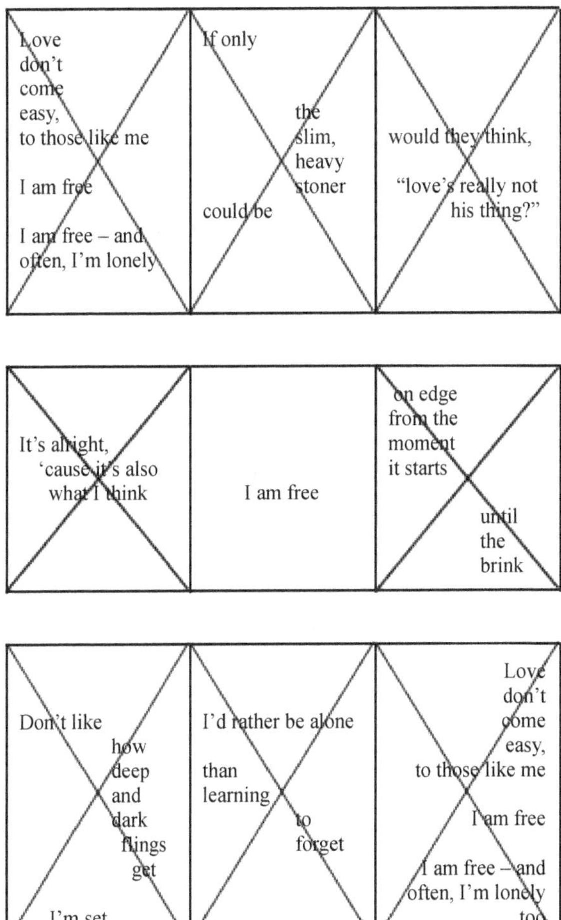
Love
don't
come
easy,
to those like me

I am free

I am free – and
often, I'm lonely
If only

the
slim,
heavy
stoner
could be
would they think,

"love's really not
his thing?"
It's alright,
'cause it's also
what I think
I am free
on edge
from the
moment
it starts

until
the
brink
Don't like
how
deep
and
dark
things
get

I'm set
I'd rather be alone

than
learning

to
forget
Love
don't
come
easy,
to those like me

I am free

I am free – and
often, I'm lonely
too

<u>*I Tried*</u>

You're drawn to me, but it's me who runs back; especially on days when growing is more painful than wilting into the sense of home I've created in your memory.

Unending tugs, on heartstrings I swear I've cut time and time again.

Your ghost passing through the walls of my consciousness – this form of intimacy the closest we'll ever be again.

Being, now a form of coping with suppressed pleas for acknowledgment,
of what you did to me and I to you – truth.

Young and vulnerable, incapable of being honorable in what we said and meant and in how we spread and our intent.

Fevered to repent sins bestowed upon us, though not ours to wear – but we placed them carefully on each other's bodies as if

I carried yours, and you carried mine, the weight would subside over time.

Fitting puzzle pieces, where they did not belong, as if we were primed to be each other's saviors.

We burned quicker than the fires surrounding cities we love.

It's fine, because wounds mend with time – I just wish the result would have lived up to the vision and not an annex of my heart from yours.

But hearts endure, and I've made it out the forest – even if you ignored us, and by us, I mean me.

We were a team, with a player broken and one who had chosen not to show up for the season endgame, because, as he proclaimed:

"I tried to love you. I really did. But I just couldn't."

...

<u>*[un]seen*</u>

One day I'll gain favor for fervor
unfettered and bold – magnetic and bubbling
and when seen, I won't fold

...

...

clear as day, I set intentions

blue waters surrounding paradise
yet, you hesitate

trudging in the murky shallows
of cost and benefit

better it be to weather storms alone,
typhoons of loneliness,
than setting proposals untrue

unseen I will float
plankton to your eyes
unseen I will feel
atoms bursting
unseen I will fare
aimless

...

Waters of Myself

<pre>
              swelling with
Waters of myself,   the moon,   to know where   foreign shores
                           make it hard   I start and the   begin.

                rain washes   surface. Sirens wail   so I keep it surface.
        cycles,   my oscillating   scaring sailors,
    Saline

Few   little can   unburdened,   is not to blame
      and very   withstand   I remain   as the cold and deep   for wreckage
                these depths.   of the unprepared.

              in that order.   always to remain
          and freeze,   Unkempt by anything,   untouched.
    Trenches crush

Warm   invite,   the torrential
      shallows but we all   that follow   come when   ignored
            understand   Cyclones   warnings are   of
                their potential.   the

                                              g e n t l e.
</pre>

<u>*'enough'*</u>

enough is *enough*

. . .

six years later

. . .

enough is *enough*

. . .

It's the 7th year, I say *'enough'*

. . .

he said, *'enough'*
Today's the day

. . .

I've had enough
I cannot settle or subdue myself much longer
Today's the day

. . .

I've had *enough*
Picking myself up from resounding desperation
Today's the day

. . .

I've had *enough*

. . .

Today's the day
I've had *enough*

. . .

For I am, have been, & will always be

. . .

It's the 7th year, I say *'enough'*

. . .

enough is *enough*

. . .

six years later

. . .

enough
is

enough!

I've had *enough* of the nothing,
to the point where black holes formed in my marrow.
A polka-dot paradise on skeletal remains.

enough!
You've said *enough* with the bitter nothings kept from my ear.
Resounding, my temples ache in your silent roar.

enough!

I've had *enough* of the cattle-calls herding pretense to its keeper.
Gifted to me, in attempts to weaken my spirit;
and you've won.

But,
enough is *enough*!

For I am, have been, and always will be.
Even on days when I refuse to believe it.

enough!

enough!

. . .

'enough'

<u>*Weird-Heavy*</u>

There's this weird-heavy sense of me, felt recently –
like a pressure change as twisters form, right before they
begin to lift and, I too, in the winds am drifting; astray
… … … … …   There's this weird-heavy sense of me, felt
recently – like looming clouds made of cotton, over waves,
receding past reefs, right before they roar back – oh, so
gracefully – and land on all they could never
reach before, leaving it, catatonic   … … … … …
There's this weird-heavy sense of me, felt
recently – reminiscent to tremors –
… … shaking faults back to reality
with resounding trumpets,
as volcanic symphonies
devour oceans of
myself they were,
never meant to
to meet – leaving
remnants,
of the land,
land I call,
my
body
….
…
…
…
.
.
.
.
.
.
.

.
...
It's
raining,
the clouds
are more grey,
weird, and heavy,
than feelings I've carried
inside for the last six years.
Raindrops palpitate… like my
heart once used to, uncontrollably,
as smells of moisture-filled soil and
creosote, flood the air. No rose, but I'm
picked to feel existence prick as the rain
picks up. Lemon lavender tea fills me with
this warmth I haven't felt in ages, and oil
spills of reluctance diminish with every flash
highlighting the sky. Trees sway, and I am
overwhelmed with content. Clouds carried
underneath, my eyes, join the orchestral
pulsing of nature. I can feel my troubles
wash away. I feel the weird-heavy sense
of me lift, and once again, I begin to
feel whole. I wish I could walk
into the clouds and be
lost – forever.

<u>*Saturn Returns (27)*</u>

s-
h-
ell-
shoc-
ked to
find the
shell I
used
to fit in.
gle
am-
ing
tiny
pearl,
that I am. displayed.
tarnished outer layers
still show the grooves of
existence, but no longer
do I fit. won't let anyone
string me along, or knot
my stomach. delicate
 material not meant to be
digested. leave you – –
– – – – foaming at the
mouth, like seas which
gave rise to myself and
Aphrodite. I too, an Ares
– like her lover. April
showers cover my skin,
and my kin will always
know me – no matter
state or place I'm in. …
revel in me – 27. let
Saturn return
to symphonies.

Don't let them destroy you,
ethereal and everlasting – made of the same materials
which formed the cosmos, making you a star.
Majestic and magnificent – shaped of strength and power.
Know, in softness you'll go far, for you are refined and reverent;
the physical embodiment of what it means to love.

As first of the cycle,
burn in furry and
be volcanic in temperance.
of the cosmos,
fall with honor into grace
and rise from the ashes.
clouds within you will
bring life, again – and
you will reign.
constellation that you are,
my sun;
a star.

<u>*Beautiful, again*</u>

I can make this place beautiful, again

I know I can – with enough soil to sustain
and moisture to grow

                             I can make this place beautiful, again

                        I know I can – with an inch of rain and the
                                       sun to unfold me

I can make this place beautiful, again

I know I can – with enough passing days
like mother knew I could

                             I can make this place beautiful, again

                  I know I can – created of her and from her wounds

In the end,
I will give back everything I took

                    . . .

<u>Sunflower</u>   *I'll plant*
                    sunflowers   for
              you,   my means   for sur-
                 vival. like soil   you   keep
                  me rooted on days   when
              the   winds   blow harshest
              against the   back of my
         stem. Your   undying
               love covers   my leaves in a
               blanket of   tolerance to
          pests, heat, and stigma; like that
             of the female flower they
                 feverishly try to
                     uncover.
   My rays shine   – in
           beauty, for that which you
              provide is enough to
                    sustain me
                    with
                    everlasting
                    happiness. Seeds of joy
              I will sow, in remembrance
              of the   day you picked
              me;   though
              not
              fully
              bloo-
              med
              you
              saw
              the
              radi-
              ance
              I'd
              achieve.
              For
              you,
              I have
              always
         been enough.

<u>*Sunny Days*</u>

Sunny day
beams accompany
the breeze. It's spring days
like these that let me feel my body
– grounded. Happy trees look
greener.
Bird sing melodies in
harmony to mine. Pollen fills the
air and I sneeze, with appreciation.
Life feels lite today –
I'm unencumbered,
taking in the world around me. It's been far too long,
since I've had
gratitude
for
l
i
f
e

…

I see myself in you,
but never will you have to fumble
as I did

Jesus is your kin, my darling
You are divinely protected

1st

Sweet girl,
your smile lets me know you are endless
in abundance and love

Your presence is the sweetness of the spring,
after a winter's frost

2nd

Subsequent to tragedy,
you're meant to be for us, and us for thee

You'll complete the trinity,
like your father, because the best things
come in sets of three

3rd

Sweet children,
my love will always be for you
– unconditioned –
I'll teach you all too, to keep the torch alive

Here's to,
the
2nd generation

. . .

Mother

                        I have a memory I can't quite place.
        Hollowing – cleaving out space between ribs. In my cage, a tall reflection effaced of all features leans back – unwilling to embrace. For grace is a virtue seldom shown to those of us who shine bold and amaze.

Mother,
please, hold me as I weep. Scarred belly, that from which I rose, like the name of your mother, Rosa. A flower so beautiful she couldn't be kept from her savior.
                               Recently,
I've felt heartbreak I know to be hers, for she never got to be.

Mother,
you never had one, but I wish you'd learned to be. For my siblings, yourself, and mostly me. For at least, they've had my childish guidance.
                  And I'm sorry if
this poem brings you anguish but I hope you can see that the child you thought you knew, much like your brother, never got to be. Eight-years-old and six feet deep in his psyche's depleted state.
              I hope to one day fix fixed fixations placed on me, through thought-patterns taught and thought rejected on decree, that that youth so bold with an eye so keen, foretold. Given gifts of compassion and strength, who foresaw grief to come.

Kingdoms to reign will come,
like moisture that rain in the desert brings – seldom, but always when needed.
                  Mother,
I have a memory I can't quite place. This pain, a visceral sight pricked between brows you taught me to pluck – like my wings – so that I'd never fly away. I'm sorry shrouding truth is a gift I was never given.

                     . . .

Left ear to the heavens as her voice rings.

On days when I fly too close to the sun she brings those rains,
again. Not to cloud my judgment, but to avert the collector's gaze.
And though we've never met – I praise her.

Jesus,
my name and what a lovely cross to bear – seer of truth and fair
fickle heart.

I have a memory I can't quite place,
for I know it's yet to come. The day we replace love lost, in
action's haste, roses will once again bloom on grandmother's grave
– and the gravity will lift. Letting us save what we thought once
lost.

Mother, I hope for once you'll listen without aim.
Mother,
I understand your well-intentioned nature.
but
Mother,
I need you to face your demons. So, you can face the child – your
child – who never got to be.

. . .

But all in due time.